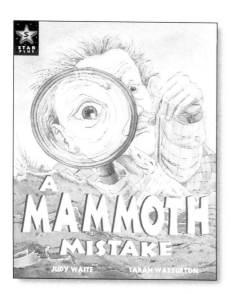

The front cover

What do you think this story might be about?

What clues are there in the illustration?

Who could the person on the front cover be?

The back cover

Let's read the blurb together.

What do you think the 'mammoth' mistake might be?

The title page

What is happening in this picture?

What other clues does it give us about the story?

1

Lesson 1 (Chapter 1)

Read pages 2 to 5

Purpose: To find out why Rachel goes on an archaeological dig.

Pause at page 5

What does Rachel's thought bubble tell us?

What did Dad think?

What type of tool could Monty be?

Chapter 1

It all began when Dad saw the advertisement in the paper:

> **CHILDREN'S ARCHAEOLOGICAL DIG**
> PLACES STILL AVAILABLE.
> COME AND WORK WITH A HIGHLY QUALIFIED ARCHAEOLOGIST.
> YOU COULD DISCOVER THE TREASURES OF AN ANCIENT WORLD!
> **CALL PROFESSOR NORMAN**
> **ON: 02012 567 890**
> AFTER ALL, YOU NEVER KNOW …

"This looks good, Rachel," said Dad. "It'll give you something to do over the holidays."

"What's wrong with watching television?" I asked.

Dad frowned. "You need to be out in the fresh air," he said.

"I don't like arky-whatsit-things. They're boring," I said.

"You liked that museum I took you to last summer," Dad said.

I didn't answer. The truth was, I had NOT liked the museum. The only good thing had been the gift shop. I'd bought Monty there.

Monty was a little carved woolly mammoth made about fourteen thousand years ago.

Well, he wasn't really that old. He was just a copy of a tool ancient people had used. The real one was in the museum inside a glass case. I kept mine in his plastic display box.

I gave Dad a 'take pity on me' look. It didn't work.

At ten o'clock the next morning, I was on an archaeological dig. I took Monty with me.

Read pages 6 to 9

Purpose: To find out if Rachel enjoyed the dig when she got there.

Pause at page 9

What sort of things do you think Professor Norman expected to find?

Why did Professor Norman dislike Rachel? Find evidence in the text to support your answer. (*You won't get me digging around in that!*)

Rachel spoke without thinking. Have you ever said anything you wish you hadn't?

Right from the start, I didn't get on with Professor Norman. He had bought this site, a crumbling old house with a huge overgrown garden, because it was of great archaeological interest.

"It is surprising how much we can learn from old things, even something like ancient rubbish," Professor Norman told us, soon after we arrived.

All of the other children looked very interested. They looked as if they wouldn't mind at all being up to their elbows in ancient rubbish.

I couldn't help it. My thoughts just sort of jumped out of my mouth.

"Yuck!" I said. "You won't get me digging around in that!"

Professor Norman glared at me. After that he began to pick on me. He gave me the dirtiest, most boring jobs to do.

Read pages 10 to 11
Purpose: To find out if Rachel makes a discovery.

Pause at page 11
Why had Rachel brought Monty?

Why did Rachel decide to have lunch by herself?

Please turn to page 14 for Revisit and Respond activities.

By lunchtime, I was really fed up. I sat on my own, munching my sandwiches. The only company I had was Monty. I'd brought him so I could ask Professor Norman questions about him. Except that, after Professor Norman had been so horrible, I didn't feel like asking him anything.

I took Monty out of his display box. The label on the box said that he was a tool that ancient people had used for hunting. Perhaps he could hunt out some ancient treasure for me now.

"Time to get back to work!" said Professor Norman. "Get the wheelbarrow. We've got piles of mud to move."

"Oh, no . . ." I began, but Professor Norman glared at me again, and I changed my mind. I quickly slipped Monty into my pocket. Then I went to get the wheelbarrow. That's when the real trouble began.

Lesson 2 (Chapter 2)

Recap lesson 1

Who are the two main characters in the story? (*Rachel and Professor Norman*) How do they feel about each other?

How was Rachel feeling at the end of Chapter 1?

Re-read the last sentence on page 11. What do you think will happen next?

Read pages 12 to 15

Purpose: To confirm predictions.

Pause at page 15

Why does Professor Norman want Rachel to stand back?

What mistake is Professor Norman about to make?

Why does Rachel feel sick?

Why is the word 'finds' on page 14 written between quote marks? Use the clues in the picture to help you. How does this add to the humour of the story?

Chapter 2

Everyone started digging again. Then, suddenly, one of the children shouted, "I've found some sort of ornament!" He was holding something small and muddy. I knew right away what it was. Monty had fallen out of my pocket into the mud.

Still, it shouldn't have been a problem. Professor Norman would know that Monty was only a copy. I walked forward, about to ask for him back.

"Stand back," growled Professor Norman. "This could be the find of the century."

Professor Norman carefully lifted Monty with a pair of tweezers.

He carried Monty to the table that was set up for 'finds' at the edge of the garden. He stared at Monty through a magnifying glass.

I was feeling sick. Any minute now Professor Norman would realize he'd been tricked and come roaring back.

Read pages 16 to 19

Purpose: To find out what Professor Norman does with his find.

Pause at page 19

Why didn't Professor Norman listen to Rachel?

Why did Professor Norman ring the television news?

How did he feel when Rachel owned up about Monty? What words tell you? (*he wished I was about fourteen thousand years away*)

Look at the illustration on page 18. How has the illustrator added humour to the picture?

That didn't happen. Instead, Professor Norman hurried over with his mobile phone in his hand.

"This is an amazing find," he said. "I've called the television news. They'll be here soon."

I tried to tell him then, I really did.
"Professor Norman, I . . ."
"Hurry up and get back to work," Professor Norman said to me. "This is my big chance. I want this to look like a busy site, where everyone is happy."
"But I just . . ."

At that moment, a man and woman appeared. The man was carrying a TV camera. Professor Norman rubbed his hands together.
"Welcome," he said. "I'm sure your viewers will want to know about this story . . ."
I couldn't stand it any longer. Apart from anything else, I wanted Monty back.

"Actually," I said loudly, "he's mine."

Professor Norman looked at me as if he wished I was about fourteen thousand years away. The TV people smiled kindly, but they kept on setting up the camera.
"I can prove it." I showed them the plastic box, and pointed to the label.

Wesley Hill Museum
Copy of an ancient hunting tool carved
from reindeer antler.

READ

Read pages 20 to the end

Purpose: To find out if Rachel got into trouble.

PAUSE

Pause at page 24

Why did the television people want to talk to Professor Norman?

What did Rachel find out at the end of the day? (*she liked digging to find things*)

The TV people didn't look pleased. They'd been dragged all this way just for Monty. Professor Norman looked even less pleased.

"I want my mammoth back," I said.

Professor Norman glared at me. He threw Monty down on the ground, then he ran up the garden and into the house.

And that put an end to our day. The TV people were still there when I left. I guess they wanted to talk to Professor Norman again. Although it wouldn't be the kind of news story he'd wanted.

Dad said that perhaps I would have had more fun watching TV after all. The funny thing was, I didn't want to. Instead, I went out into the warm summer evening with Monty and a wheelbarrow, and began digging.

After all, you never know . . .

After Reading

Revisit and Respond

Lesson 1

- (T) What clue does the author gives us that something is going to happen? (Page 11: *That's when the real trouble began.*)
- (T) Ask the children to predict what will happen in Chapter 2.
- (T) Ask the children to look at the beginning of the book again. Ask them for words to describe Dad.

Lesson 2

- **T** Why did the author choose to call the story *A Mammoth Mistake?* (Make sure the children understand the two meanings of 'mammoth' in the title, ie a big mistake, and a mistake over a mammoth.)

- **T** Ask the children to say what type of story this is. Is it a traditional tale, a humorous story, a suspense story? Can they think of any other humorous stories they have read? (*The School Concert*)

- **T** Ask the children to compare *The School Concert* and *A Mammoth Mistake*. What is funny in *The School Concert*? (*Jazz says funny things and uses humorous descriptions, e.g. like a big blue fish.*)
  What is funny in *A Mammoth Mistake*? (*the situation*)

- **S** Ask the children to read page 20 out loud, using the punctuation to help them read with expression.

Follow-up

Independent Group Activity Work

This book is accompanied by two photocopy masters, one with a reading focus, and one with a writing focus, which support the main teaching objectives of this book. The photocopy masters can be found in the Planning and Assessment Guide.

PCM 11 (*reading*)
PCM 12 (*writing*)

Writing

Guided writing: Write an imaginary interview between the reporter and Professor Norman. Use PCM 12 for support.

Extended writing: Write a short conversation between Rachel and her dad. What will Rachel tell him about her day? What will Dad say?

Assessment Points

Assess that the children have learnt the main teaching points of the book by checking that they can:

- compare books by different authors on a similar theme
- respond to humorous stories
- use punctuation to read with expression.

- **There is a Comprehension Assessment Sheet linked to this book. (See *Planning and Assessment Guide*)**